On It, Phonics! Vowel Sounds

# This Is Ten

## The Short E Sound

By Connor Stratton

level 1 little blue readers

www.littlebluehousebooks.com



Little Blue House is distributed by North Star Editions:
sales@northstareditions.com | 888-417-0195

Produced for Little Blue House by Red Line Editorial.

Reading Consultant: Andrew P. Johnson, PhD, Distinguished Faculty Scholar and Professor of Literacy Instruction, Minnesota State University, Mankato

Photographs ©: iStockphoto, cover, 5 (bell), 5 (men), 5 (pen), 5 (ten), 6, 9 (top), 9 (bottom), 19, 21 (bottom), 23; Shutterstock Images, 5 (egg), 5 (end), 5 (pet), 5 (smell), 5 (wet), 11 (top), 11 (bottom), 13 (top), 13 (bottom), 15, 17 (top), 17 (bottom), 21 (top)

**Library of Congress Control Number: 2023909946**

**ISBN**
978-1-64619-923-5 (hardcover)
978-1-64619-941-9 (paperback)
978-1-64619-976-1 (ebook pdf)
978-1-64619-959-4 (hosted ebook)

Printed in the United States of America
Mankato, MN
102023

# About the Author

Connor Stratton writes and edits nonfiction children's books. He lives in Minnesota.

# Table of Contents

# Consultant Note

"On It, Phonics!" is designed to reinforce vowel sounds, beginning blends, and sight words and to provide reading practice for young readers. Books like these are one important part of a comprehensive literacy program for students at emergent and beginning levels. "On It, Phonics!" should be used with other high-quality children's books. Instructors and parents are advised to go over the words in the picture glossary before students begin reading, and review the sight words after students finish reading. You can also ask students to go back and identify words with the target letter-sound.

Andrew P. Johnson, PhD,
Distinguished Faculty Scholar and
Professor of Literacy Instruction,
Minnesota State University, Mankato

# Short E Picture Glossary

**bell**

**egg**

**end**

**hen**

**men**

**pen**

**pet**

**smell**

**ten**

**wet**

10

# Ten

This is ten.

There are ten men.

men

men

There are ten bells.

bell

bell

This is a pet.

This pet is wet.

This pet can smell.

pet
wet

smell
pet

There are ten pets.

This is a hen.

This hen is in a pen.

hen

pen
hen

Ten hens are in this pen.

This is an egg.

This hen has eggs.

There are ten eggs.

hen
egg

egg

This is the end.

7

# Sight Words

| | |
|---|---|
| a | in |
| an | is |
| are | the |
| can | there |
| has | this |